DEDICATION

I humbly dedicate this work to the supreme spiritual being.

TABLE OF CONTENTS

ACKNOWLEDGMENTS

As I sit here reflecting on the journey that has led to the creation of *Mastering Fortran*, I am filled with profound gratitude for the incredible individuals and communities that have made this book possible. This endeavor has not just been about writing—it's been about sharing a powerful tool that has shaped my own path and continues to change the world of scientific and high-performance computing.

To my mentors, whose wisdom and encouragement have shaped my understanding of Fortran and programming at large, I owe you a debt that words can scarcely repay. Your insights into both the technical and philosophical aspects of coding have been invaluable. Your patience in answering questions, your willingness to challenge my assumptions, and your unwavering belief in the transformative potential of this language have inspired me to write this book, not just as a guide, but as a legacy for those who wish to unlock the power of Fortran.

A special note of appreciation goes to the entire Fortran community, whose contributions, discussions, and innovations have continuously pushed the boundaries of what this language can do. Your collaboration and tireless pursuit of excellence fuel the ongoing evolution of Fortran. It's through your collective efforts that Fortran remains one of the most effective and enduring tools in scientific computing. This book stands as a testament to the shared knowledge and passion that drives our field forward.

To my readers—whether you are just starting your Fortran journey or are looking to sharpen your advanced skills—this book is for you. You are the reason this book exists. I wrote it with you in mind, and I wrote it for you. Your curiosity, your ambition, and your thirst for knowledge inspire me to continue exploring new frontiers in programming. I have no doubt that the skills and insights you gain from this book will not only enhance your career but will also ignite new passions within you. With each line of code you write, you become part of a larger, transformative movement that shapes the future of science, engineering, and technology.

To the teams, colleagues, and peers who have supported me along the way, thank you for your feedback, your encouragement, and your steadfast belief in the importance of this work. Your contributions have refined this book and ensured that it is not only a tool but also an experience. Your thoughtful perspectives have ensured that this work transcends the theoretical and becomes deeply practical, allowing it to resonate in real-world applications.

The pages that follow are not just a collection of concepts and examples—they are an invitation. An invitation to challenge the limits of your imagination, to discover new possibilities, and to push the boundaries of what you can accomplish. As you read and apply the lessons in this book, know that you are not just learning to write code; you are gaining the power to solve problems, to innovate, and to make a tangible impact in your field.

As you embark on your own Fortran journey, remember that every line of code you write is a step towards mastery. There will be moments of triumph, moments of frustration, and moments of awe. Embrace them all. It's through these experiences that you will truly begin to understand the depth of your own potential.

Thank you for choosing to take this journey with me. Your dedication to mastering Fortran will not only enrich your professional life but also empower you to contribute to a community of innovators who are shaping the future. I'm honored to be part of that journey with you.

Let's begin.

CHAPTER 1
Introduction to Fortran

Fortran, short for "Formula Translation," is a language that has stood the test of time. Born in the early 1950s, it was designed to address the growing need for high-performance numerical computing, especially in the realms of science, engineering, and research. Even after decades of innovation in programming languages, Fortran remains an irreplaceable tool in computational science. Its efficiency in managing complex mathematical models and handling massive datasets makes it the go-to choice for many scientific applications today.

Fortran is widely used in disciplines such as:

- **Physics**: Simulating particle collisions, modeling cosmological events.

- **Engineering**: Designing aircraft, automobiles, and other systems.

- **Climate Science**: Modeling weather patterns and climate change predictions.

- **Biotechnology**: Modeling protein structures and molecular simulations.

- **Data Analytics**: Handling large-scale computations in data-driven research.

Despite the rise of newer languages, Fortran's role in high-performance computing (HPC) remains central, especially when precision, speed, and memory efficiency are critical. The language has continuously evolved to keep pace with technological advancements, making it a must-learn language for those working in these fields.

History and Evolution of Fortran

Fortran is not just a programming language—it's a cornerstone of computational science, with a legacy that spans over 70 years. Initially developed by IBM in the 1950s, Fortran became the first widely adopted high-level programming language. Each subsequent revision has kept it competitive with modern needs while preserving backward compatibility.

Key milestones in Fortran's evolution include:

- **Fortran 66 (1966)**: The first standardized version, which made Fortran more consistent and portable across platforms.

- **Fortran 77 (1978)**: Introduced structured programming concepts like DO loops and IF-ELSE statements, significantly improving code readability and maintainability.

- **Fortran 90/95**: Brought major updates like modular programming, dynamic arrays, and better array handling, making it a powerful tool for modern scientific work.

- **Fortran 2003/2008**: Introduced object-oriented features and interoperability with C, ensuring Fortran's relevance in complex software ecosystems.

- **Fortran 2018**: This version added further modernizations, such as coarrays for parallel programming, making Fortran a robust tool for multi-core processors and distributed computing.

Each iteration has made Fortran faster, more versatile, and more adaptable to modern computational needs, ensuring that it remains one of the most reliable languages for high-performance computing.

Strengths of Fortran in High-Performance Computing
Fortran's enduring success in high-performance computing (HPC) lies in its optimization for numerical computing. Some of the key strengths include:

1. **Optimization for Computational Performance**: Fortran compilers are highly efficient at optimizing numerical and array-based computations. The language was designed with computational efficiency in mind, enabling it to perform better in tasks that require large-scale matrix operations, solving differential equations, and other data-intensive processes.

2. **Parallel Computing**: Fortran 2018 introduced **Coarrays**, a feature that allows you to write parallel code with minimal changes to the existing code structure. Coarrays are an advanced feature that simplifies parallel computing, allowing Fortran to scale effectively on modern multi-core processors and distributed computing systems.

3. **Memory Efficiency**: Fortran's strict handling of memory layouts, particularly for multidimensional arrays, makes it one

of the most efficient languages in terms of memory management. Unlike many modern languages, Fortran allows low-level access to memory, giving you greater control over performance optimization.

4. **Legacy Systems and Integration**: Many legacy scientific applications have been written in Fortran, and these systems continue to be maintained and optimized. Fortran's ability to interface with other languages, such as C and Python, ensures its role in modern interdisciplinary research and development projects.

5. **Scientific Libraries**: Fortran boasts a rich ecosystem of scientific libraries, like LAPACK (Linear Algebra PACKage) and BLAS (Basic Linear Algebra Subprograms), which have been optimized over decades to perform highly efficient mathematical operations.

Preparing Your Environment

Before writing your first Fortran program, it's essential to set up your development environment. This involves installing a compiler, choosing an IDE (Integrated Development Environment), and understanding how to compile and run your code.

Choosing the Right Compiler

Choosing the right compiler is vital for maximizing performance and compatibility. The two most commonly used Fortran compilers are:

- **GFortran**: Open-source and available across different platforms (Linux, macOS, Windows). It is fully compatible with modern   Fortran   standards   (e.g.,   Fortran 90/95/2003/2008/2018).

- **Intel Fortran Compiler (IFORT)**: A proprietary compiler known for its performance optimization. It provides features such as vectorization and multi-threading, making it ideal for high-performance computing tasks.

Installing GFortran and Intel Fortran

1. **GFortran** Installation:

    o **Linux**: sudo apt-get install gfortran

    o **macOS**: Use Homebrew: brew install gcc

    o **Windows**: Install via MinGW or download a precompiled binary.

2. **Intel Fortran** Installation:

    o Download the compiler from Intel's official site.

    o Follow the installation wizard for your operating system.

Once installed, both compilers come with tools for compiling and debugging your Fortran code.

Writing, Compiling, and Running Your First Program

1. Open a text editor and write the following simple Fortran program in a new file named hello.f90:

```
PROGRAM HelloWorld
  PRINT *, "Hello, World!"
END PROGRAM HelloWorld
```

2. Compile the Program:

- ○ **GFortran**: gfortran hello.f90 -o hello

- ○ **Intel Fortran**: ifort hello.f90 -o hello

3. Run the Program:

- ○ **Linux/macOS**: ./hello

- ○ **Windows**: hello.exe

Reflective Questions

- Why is Fortran still used in high-performance computing today, despite the emergence of other programming languages?

- What are some of the scientific domains that benefit most from Fortran's numerical computing capabilities?

- In your opinion, how does the parallel programming feature in Fortran 2018, Coarrays, compare to similar features in other languages like OpenMP or MPI?

- How would you use Fortran to solve a complex problem in your field of interest? Can you outline the potential computational challenges and how Fortran would address them?

Interactive Exercise

1. **Exercise 1: Setting Up Your Development Environment**

    - ○ Follow the installation steps outlined above to install GFortran or Intel Fortran on your system.

    - ○ Write your first simple Fortran program (hello.f90) and compile it.

- o Reflect on the process: What challenges did you encounter during installation? How did you resolve them?

2. **Exercise 2: Understanding the Strengths of Fortran**

   - o Research an example of a large scientific simulation that utilizes Fortran.

   - o Explain the computational tasks involved and how Fortran's features (such as array handling or coarrays) make it ideal for such simulations.

3. **Exercise 3: Writing More Complex Programs**

   - o Modify the "Hello, World!" program to print your name and the current date.

   - o Add a loop to print your name 5 times in a row.

Key Takeaways

- **Fortran's Long Legacy**: Fortran has been a foundational language in scientific computing for over seven decades, continually evolving to meet modern computational needs.

- **High-Performance Computing**: The language's strong performance in numerical computations and array-based operations makes it indispensable in fields like physics, engineering, and climate science.

- **Modern Features**: New versions of Fortran, like Fortran 2018, introduce modern features such as Coarrays for parallel programming, keeping it competitive with newer languages.

- **Scientific Libraries**: Fortran has a wealth of optimized libraries that make it a powerful tool for solving complex mathematical problems.

CHAPTER 2
Fortran Basics: The Building Blocks

In this chapter, we will focus on the essential building blocks of Fortran, enabling you to start writing functional programs with solid understanding. We will cover the structure of a Fortran program, data types, variables, constants, and the core input/output operations in Fortran. These are the foundation stones of any program, and mastering them will allow you to build more complex and powerful applications. By the end of this chapter, you will be comfortable with the basic elements of Fortran and be ready to dive into more advanced topics.

Structure of a Fortran Program
1.1 Program Structure

A Fortran program typically follows a specific structure, including the following parts:

- **Program Header**: The keyword PROGRAM is used to define the beginning of a program, followed by the program name.

- **Declarations**: Here, you declare variables and specify their types.

- **Executable Statements**: These are the instructions that the program will execute, such as calculations or displaying output.

- **End Program**: The keyword END PROGRAM marks the end of the program.

Example:

```
PROGRAM HelloWorld
  PRINT *, 'Hello, World!'
END PROGRAM HelloWorld
```

This is a simple Fortran program that prints "Hello, World!" to the console.

Explanation:

- **PROGRAM HelloWorld**: Declares the start of the program with the name HelloWorld.

- **PRINT *, 'Hello, World!'**: Outputs the text "Hello, World!" to the screen.

- **END PROGRAM HelloWorld**: Indicates the end of the program.

Data Types and Variables
1.2 Understanding Data Types

Fortran is a strongly typed language, meaning that variables must be declared with specific types. These data types determine what kind of values a variable can hold and how much memory it consumes. Here are the most common Fortran data types:

- **Integers**: Represent whole numbers.

- **Reals**: Represent floating-point numbers (decimals).

- **Complex Numbers**: Used for representing complex numbers (real + imaginary part).

- **Logical**: Used for boolean values (True or False).

- **Character**: Used for text or strings.

1.3 Declaring Variables

Variables in Fortran are declared using a TYPE keyword, followed by the variable name and optionally its size (for arrays).

Example:

```
INTEGER :: x
REAL :: pi
LOGICAL :: flag
CHARACTER(20) :: message
```

- **INTEGER :: x**: Declares an integer variable named x.

- **REAL :: pi**: Declares a real variable named pi.

- **LOGICAL :: flag**: Declares a logical (boolean) variable named flag.

- **CHARACTER(20) :: message**: Declares a character variable message that can hold up to 20 characters.

Constants and Parameters
1.4 Defining Constants

Fortran allows you to define constants that do not change during the program's execution. These can be defined using the **PARAMETER** keyword.

Example:

```
REAL, PARAMETER :: pi = 3.14159
INTEGER, PARAMETER :: max_size = 100
```

- **REAL, PARAMETER :: pi = 3.14159** declares a constant pi with the value 3.14159.

- **INTEGER, PARAMETER :: max_size = 100** declares a constant max_size with the value 100.

Why Use Constants?

Constants help in improving program readability and maintainability. For example, if you used pi in multiple places in your program, changing its value would be cumbersome if it were not defined as a constant. Using constants makes code more reliable and easier to update.

Basic Input and Output Operations

1.5 Writing to the Console

Fortran provides several ways to output information to the console using the PRINT statement.

Example:

```
PRINT *, 'The value of pi is: ', pi
```

Here, pi is a variable, and **PRINT** * is the basic syntax for outputting information to the console.

1.6 Reading from the Console

You can accept user input through the READ statement. This allows you to assign values to variables dynamically during program execution.

Example:

```
INTEGER :: num
PRINT *, 'Enter a number:'
READ *, num
PRINT *, 'You entered: ', num
```

- **The READ *,** num reads an integer value from the console and stores it in the variable num.

- The program then prints out the value entered by the user.

Common Troubleshooting Tips

When you first start programming in Fortran, you might encounter some common errors or issues. Here are a few that new programmers often face:

- **Error: Variable not declared**: Ensure that you declare all variables before using them.

  - ○ Solution: Use the IMPLICIT NONE statement at the beginning of the program to ensure that all variables are explicitly declared.

- **Mismatched data types**: For example, trying to assign a real value to an integer variable.

  - ○ Solution: Check your variable types and ensure they match the type of data you are working with.

Interactive Exercise

Exercise 1: Your First Program

Write a Fortran program that:

1. Prints a welcome message.

2. Accepts the user's name and age.

3. Prints a personalized message saying, "Hello, [name]! You are [age] years old."

Hint: Use the READ statement to accept user input and PRINT to display the output.

Exercise 2: Working with Constants

Create a Fortran program that calculates the area of a circle, using the formula area = pi * radius^2, where pi is a constant and radius is a user input.

Hint: Use REAL, PARAMETER for the constant and READ to get the radius from the user.

Key Takeaways

- **Program Structure**: A Fortran program has a simple structure with a PROGRAM header, executable statements, and an END PROGRAM statement.

- **Data Types**: Fortran supports various data types, including integers, reals, complex numbers, logicals, and characters.

- **Variables and Constants**: Variables store data, and constants provide unchanging values that can be used across the program.

- **Input and Output**: PRINT is used to display information, while READ allows you to accept user input.

- **Troubleshooting**: Common issues include undeclared variables and data type mismatches. The IMPLICIT NONE statement is useful for avoiding undeclared variables.

Reflective Questions

1. What would happen if you try to print a character variable without first declaring it?

2. Why is it important to use constants in your programs? How does it help with program maintenance?

3. What are the differences between real and complex numbers? Can you think of a situation where you would use
   complex numbers in scientific programming?

CHAPTER 3
Control Structures: Directing Program Flow

In this chapter, we will explore how to control the flow of your Fortran programs using different types of control structures. These are fundamental concepts in programming, and understanding them will allow you to write flexible, efficient, and readable code. We will break down each topic with clear explanations and practical examples that illustrate their real-world applications. By the end of this chapter, you will be able to use conditional statements, loops, and special flow control commands confidently.

Introduction to Control Structures in Fortran

Control structures in Fortran dictate the flow of the program execution. In other words, they control the sequence in which statements are executed based on certain conditions or repeated until certain conditions are met. This is crucial because most real-world problems require decisions (conditional logic) and repetitive tasks (loops).

Fortran, being one of the oldest programming languages still in use today, has a rich set of control structures that have evolved over time, especially with the Fortran 90, 95, 2003, and 2018 standards. In this chapter, we'll explore the most commonly used control structures:

- **Conditional Statements** (IF, ELSE, SELECT CASE)

- **Loop Constructs** (DO, DO WHILE)

- **Control Flow Modifiers** (EXIT, CYCLE)

Conditional Statements

Conditional statements allow a program to decide which action to take based on whether a condition is true or false. In Fortran, there are two main ways to handle conditional logic: the IF statement and the SELECT CASE statement.

2.1. IF and ELSE

The IF statement evaluates a condition, and if that condition is true, it executes a block of code. If the condition is false, the program can either do nothing (in the case of an IF without an ELSE) or execute an alternative block of code (with an ELSE).

Syntax:

```
IF (condition) THEN
    ! Code block to execute if condition is true
ELSE
    ! Code block to execute if condition is false
END IF
```

Example: Checking if a number is positive, negative, or zero

```
PROGRAM CheckSign
    INTEGER :: num

    ! Ask for user input
    PRINT *, 'Enter a number:'
    READ *, num

    IF (num > 0) THEN
        PRINT *, 'The number is positive.'
    ELSE IF (num < 0) THEN
        PRINT *, 'The number is negative.'
    ELSE
        PRINT *, 'The number is zero.'
    END IF
END PROGRAM CheckSign
```

2.2. SELECT CASE

The **SELECT CASE** statement is used for making decisions based on multiple possible values of a variable. It is a cleaner alternative to using multiple IF statements when the condition involves comparing a variable against several possible values.

Syntax:

```
SELECT CASE (expression)
   CASE (value1)
      ! Code block for value1
   CASE (value2)
      ! Code block for value2
   CASE DEFAULT
      ! Code block if no other cases match
END SELECT
```

Example: Day of the Week

```
PROGRAM DayOfWeek
   INTEGER :: day

   ! Ask for user input
   PRINT *, 'Enter a number (1-7) for the day of the week:'
   READ *, day

   SELECT CASE (day)
      CASE (1)
        PRINT *, 'Monday'
      CASE (2)
        PRINT *, 'Tuesday'
      CASE (3)
        PRINT *, 'Wednesday'
      CASE (4)
        PRINT *, 'Thursday'
      CASE (5)
        PRINT *, 'Friday'
      CASE (6)
        PRINT *, 'Saturday'
      CASE (7)
        PRINT *, 'Sunday'
```

```
    CASE DEFAULT
        PRINT *, 'Invalid input, please enter a number between 1 and 7.'
    END SELECT
END PROGRAM DayOfWeek
```

Key Takeaways for Conditional Statements:

- IF and ELSE are best for handling simple true/false conditions.

- SELECT CASE is useful when you need to check multiple specific values of a single variable.

- Make sure that your logic is clear and easy to follow for both you and anyone reading your code.

3. Loop Constructs

Loop constructs are used when a set of instructions need to be repeated multiple times. Fortran provides several loop structures, each with different use cases. The two most commonly used loops are DO loops and DO WHILE loops.

3.1. DO Loops

The DO loop is one of the simplest loops in Fortran. It repeats a block of code a specific number of times. A DO loop is typically used when the number of iterations is known before the loop begins.

Syntax:

```
DO index = start, end, increment
    ! Code block to execute
END DO
```

Example: Printing numbers from 1 to 10

```
PROGRAM PrintNumbers
    INTEGER :: i

    DO i = 1, 10
        PRINT *, i
    END DO
END PROGRAM PrintNumbers
```

3.2. DO WHILE Loops

The DO WHILE loop continues to execute a block of code as long as a specified condition is true. It's particularly useful when the number of iterations is not known in advance.

Syntax:

```
DO WHILE (condition)
    ! Code block to execute
END DO
```

Example: Guessing a Number

```
PROGRAM GuessNumber
    INTEGER :: secret, guess

    secret = 7  ! For example, the secret number is 7
    PRINT *, 'Guess the secret number between 1 and 10:'

    DO WHILE (guess /= secret)
        READ *, guess
        IF (guess /= secret) THEN
            PRINT *, 'Try again!'
        END IF
    END DO

    PRINT *, 'Congratulations! You guessed the number.'
END PROGRAM GuessNumber
```

Key Takeaways for Loops:

- DO loops are great for when you know how many times to repeat an action.

44

- DO WHILE loops are best when you need to repeat an action until a condition is met.

- Avoid infinite loops by making sure the condition will eventually be false.

4. EXIT and CYCLE Statements

The EXIT and CYCLE statements provide a way to break out of a loop or skip the current iteration, respectively. These statements are helpful for controlling the flow within loops, especially when dealing with complex conditions.

4.1. EXIT Statement

The EXIT statement immediately terminates the current loop and transfers control to the statement following the loop.

Syntax:

```
DO
  ! Some code
  IF (condition) EXIT
  ! More code
END DO
```

Example: Using EXIT to Stop Early

```
PROGRAM FindFactorial
  INTEGER :: n, result, i

  PRINT *, 'Enter a number:'
  READ *, n

  result = 1
  DO i = 1, n
    result = result * i
    IF (result > 100) EXIT  ! Exit if factorial exceeds 100
  END DO

  PRINT *, 'The factorial is ', result
```

```
END PROGRAM FindFactorial
```

4.2. CYCLE Statement

The CYCLE statement skips the current iteration of the loop and moves on to the next one.

Syntax:

```
DO
   ! Some code
   IF (condition) CYCLE
   ! More code
END DO
```

Example: Skipping Even Numbers

```
PROGRAM SkipEvenNumbers
   INTEGER :: i

   DO i = 1, 10
      IF (MOD(i, 2) == 0) CYCLE  ! Skip even numbers
      PRINT *, i
   END DO
END PROGRAM SkipEvenNumbers
```

Key Takeaways for EXIT and CYCLE:

- Use EXIT to break out of a loop when a specific condition is met.

- Use CYCLE to skip the current iteration of the loop and proceed to the next one.

Practical Examples

5.1. Generating a Fibonacci Series

The Fibonacci sequence is a series of numbers where each number is the sum of the two preceding ones. This example uses a DO loop to generate the first N numbers in the Fibonacci series.

```
PROGRAM Fibonacci
   INTEGER :: n, i
   INTEGER :: fib1, fib2, fib_next

   PRINT *, 'Enter the number of terms:'
   READ *, n

   fib1 = 0
   fib2 = 1

   PRINT *, 'Fibonacci series:'
   PRINT *, fib1, fib2

   DO i = 3, n
      fib_next = fib1 + fib2
      PRINT *, fib_next
      fib1 = fib2
      fib2 = fib_next
   END DO
END PROGRAM Fibonacci
```

5.2. Calculating Factorials

A factorial of a number is the product of all positive integers less than or equal to that number. Here's a DO loop implementation to calculate the factorial.

```
PROGRAM Factorial
   INTEGER :: n, i, result

   PRINT *, 'Enter a number:'
   READ *, n

   result = 1
   DO i = 1, n
      result = result * i
   END DO
   PRINT *, 'The factorial of ', n, ' is ', result
END PROGRAM Factorial
```

Reflective Questions

- What are some real-world situations where loops could be used in your daily work or life?

- How would you approach designing a program that handles multiple conditions with the SELECT CASE statement?

- What are the advantages and disadvantages of using EXIT and CYCLE in loops?

Interactive Exercise

1. Write a program that asks the user to input an integer and prints whether that number is a prime number or not.

2. Modify the Fibonacci program so that it uses a DO WHILE loop instead of a DO loop.

Key Takeaways

- **Conditional statements** help make decisions in your programs based on conditions.

- **Loops** allow you to repeat code multiple times until a condition is met.

- **Control flow modifiers** like EXIT and CYCLE provide more control within loops.

CHAPTER 4
Arrays and Data Structures

Arrays and data structures form the backbone of nearly every computational program, and mastering them is essential for any programmer, particularly in the field of scientific computing. Fortran, with its rich history in numerical simulations and high-performance computing, offers robust support for arrays and provides several tools to manage data efficiently. In this chapter, we'll explore the fundamentals of arrays, delve into multidimensional arrays, and examine the most common operations. Through hands-on examples like matrix multiplication and solving linear systems, you'll see how arrays become the cornerstone of computational science.

Defining and Using Arrays

What is an Array?

An **array** in Fortran is a collection of variables that share the same data type, such as integers, reals, or characters. Arrays allow you to store multiple values under a single variable name. The main advantage of using arrays is that they enable you to work with large amounts of data in a structured manner.

Declaring Arrays

Arrays are declared similarly to simple variables, but with dimensions specified. The **dimension** of an array refers to the number of indices or axes it has, such as 1D, 2D, or higher.

Here's a basic example of a **one-dimensional array**:

```
INTEGER, DIMENSION(5) :: arr
```

This defines an integer array called **arr** with 5 elements. You can also initialize it during declaration:

```
INTEGER, DIMENSION(5) :: arr = (/ 1, 2, 3, 4, 5 /)
```

Accessing Array Elements

Array elements are accessed using indices. For example, to access the third element of the array **arr**, you would use:

```
PRINT *, arr(3)
```

Fortran arrays are **1-based** by default, meaning the first element is **arr(1)**.

Common Array Operations

Fortran allows you to perform a wide variety of operations on arrays, such as element-wise addition, multiplication, and others.

Array Element-Wise Operations

```
arr1 = arr2 + arr3
```

This performs element-wise addition between two arrays of the same dimension and stores the result in **arr1**.

Array Reshaping

You can reshape arrays using the **reshape** intrinsic function:

```
arr2 = RESHAPE(arr1, shape=(/3,3/))
```

This reshapes a 1D array into a 2D array with 3 rows and 3 columns.

Multidimensional Arrays

In scientific computing, multidimensional arrays (or matrices) are frequently used to represent data such as grids, images, or even 3D volumetric data. Fortran provides excellent support for such data structures.

Declaring Multidimensional Arrays

To declare a **2D array** (matrix), you specify two dimensions. For instance:

```
REAL, DIMENSION(3, 3) :: matrix
```

This creates a 3x3 matrix. For a **3D array**, simply add an extra dimension:

```
REAL, DIMENSION(3, 3, 3) :: tensor
```

Accessing Elements of Multidimensional Arrays

Accessing elements in multidimensional arrays requires specifying multiple indices. For example:

```
matrix(2, 3)
```

This accesses the element at the second row and third column of **matrix**.

Array Slicing

Fortran allows **slicing** arrays to operate on subarrays. For example, to extract the second row of a matrix:

```
row2 = matrix(2, :)
```

This retrieves all elements in the second row of **matrix**.

Array Operations and Functions

Fortran's array-oriented nature allows for elegant and efficient manipulation of large datasets. Here are some essential array operations and built-in functions:

Intrinsic Array Functions

Fortran includes several intrinsic functions for array manipulation, such as:

- **SUM**: Returns the sum of all elements.

```
sum_value = SUM(arr)
```

- **PRODUCT**: Multiplies all elements together.

```
prod_value = PRODUCT(arr)
```

- **MAXVAL** and **MINVAL**: Return the largest and smallest values, respectively.

```
max_value = MAXVAL(arr)
```

- **RESHAPE**: Changes the shape of an array without modifying its data.

```
reshaped_array = RESHAPE(arr, shape=(/3, 2/))
```

Array Operations for Performance Optimization

For large-scale problems, performance is crucial. By leveraging **array slicing**, **parallel processing**, and **intrinsics**, you can optimize Fortran programs. For example, when solving large matrix operations, using **DO parallel loops** can significantly enhance performance by utilizing multi-core processors.

```
! Parallel matrix multiplication
DO i = 1, n, 1
  DO j = 1, m, 1
    DO k = 1, l, 1
```

```
      matrixC(i, j) = matrixC(i, j) + matrixA(i, k) * matrixB(k, j)
    END DO
  END DO
END DO
```

In the above, we can optimize further using OpenMP to parallelize the loops.

Practical Application: Matrix Multiplication

Matrix multiplication is a fundamental operation in numerical methods, and it frequently appears in scientific computing.

Matrix Multiplication in Fortran

Here's how you would perform matrix multiplication in Fortran:

```
SUBROUTINE MatrixMultiply(A, B, C, n)
  REAL, DIMENSION(n, n) :: A, B, C
  INTEGER :: i, j, k

  DO i = 1, n
    DO j = 1, n
      C(i, j) = 0.0
      DO k = 1, n
        C(i, j) = C(i, j) + A(i, k) * B(k, j)
      END DO
    END DO
  END DO

END SUBROUTINE MatrixMultiply
```

In this example, **MatrixMultiply** computes the matrix product of **A** and **B**, and stores the result in **C**. This function is highly adaptable for different-sized matrices, and can be extended to **3D matrices** or more.

Solving Linear Systems Using Arrays

In many scientific fields, solving linear systems is a routine task. Fortran makes solving such problems efficient with array-based operations. The simplest method for solving a linear system **Ax = b** is **Gaussian elimination** or **LU decomposition**.

Here's an example of solving a system using **Fortran's intrinsic function**:

Solving a Linear System

```
REAL, DIMENSION(3,3) :: A, X, B
INTEGER :: i, n
n = 3

! Example coefficients matrix A**
A = RESHAPE((/ 2.0, -1.0, 1.0, -3.0, -2.0, 4.0, 1.0, 3.0, 5.0 /), shape=(/3,3/))

! Example results vector B
B = (/ 3.0, 6.0, 7.0 /)

! Solving the system Ax = b
CALL GAUSS(A, B, X, n)
```

The **CALL GAUSS** would be a subroutine implementing **Gaussian elimination** or **LU decomposition**. This function will solve the linear system efficiently using array-based manipulations.

Reflective Questions

1. How can Fortran's advanced array manipulation features optimize large-scale scientific simulations, especially in high-performance computing?

2. What challenges might arise when working with large multidimensional arrays, and how can Fortran's memory management tools assist in these scenarios?

3. What are some real-world scenarios in climate modeling or engineering simulations where matrix multiplication and linear system solvers are crucial?

Exercise 1: Matrix Multiplication

- Write a program to multiply two matrices. Ensure that your program handles edge cases, such as mismatched dimensions.

Exercise 2: Solving Linear Systems

- Implement a Fortran program that solves a system of linear equations using Gaussian elimination.

Exercise 3: Array Operations Challenge

- Write a Fortran program to compute the dot product of two vectors using array operations. Investigate how the performance differs between using loops and direct array operations.

Key Takeaways

- **Arrays in Fortran**: Arrays can hold large datasets, and their management is vital for solving complex scientific problems. Knowing how to declare, initialize, and manipulate arrays is a core skill.

- **Multidimensional Arrays**: These are essential for handling 2D and 3D data like matrices and tensors. Mastering their use opens the door to more advanced computational methods.

- **Array Operations**: Fortran offers a wide range of functions for optimizing performance in mathematical operations, including **SUM**, **PRODUCT**, and **MAXVAL**.

- **Real-World Applications**: From climate modeling to high-performance computing, arrays play a central role in simulations and problem-solving in modern industries.

CHAPTER 5
Modular Programming in Fortran

Modular programming is a cornerstone of writing clean, efficient, and maintainable code in Fortran. By dividing complex programs into smaller, reusable units, we can enhance code organization, reduce errors, and improve readability. In this chapter, we will explore subroutines, functions, and modules, while also diving into best practices for modular programming. The chapter will introduce foundational concepts, followed by advanced insights into optimizing modular Fortran code for large-scale problems. You will learn how modular programming is essential for high-performance computing, scientific simulations, and real-world problem-solving.

Subroutines and Functions: Writing Reusable Code
Subroutines

A **subroutine** is a block of code that performs a specific task and can be called from different parts of your program. Subroutines are great for breaking down a program into logical pieces, each of which handles a specific aspect of the problem. They help make your code more modular and reusable.

Defining a Subroutine

To define a subroutine, you use the **SUBROUTINE** keyword followed by the subroutine name and the list of arguments. Here's a basic structure:

```
SUBROUTINE my_subroutine(arg1, arg2)
 INTEGER, INTENT(IN) :: arg1
 REAL, INTENT(IN) :: arg2
```

```
 ! Subroutine logic goes here
  PRINT , 'The sum is:', arg1 + arg2
 END SUBROUTINE my_subroutine
```

- **INTENT(IN)** indicates that the argument is passed by value (i.e., it cannot be modified inside the subroutine).

- **arg1** is an integer, while **arg2** is a real number.

Calling a Subroutine

Subroutines are called using the **CALL** keyword. Example:

```
CALL my_subroutine(10, 20.5)
```

functions

A **function** is similar to a subroutine, but unlike subroutines, functions return a value. Functions are typically used when you need to compute a result that will be used later in your program. Functions can be used in expressions.

Defining a Function

Here's an example of a simple function definition:

```
REAL FUNCTION add_numbers(num1,num2)
  REAL, INTENT(IN) :: num1, num2

  add_numbers = num1 + num2
END FUNCTION add_numbers
```

- The function **add_numbers** takes two real arguments and returns their sum.

Calling a Function

You call a function directly in an expression:

```
result = add_numbers(5.5, 10.2)
```

- **Subroutines** do not return a value, but can modify passed arguments.

- **Functions** return a value and can be used within expressions.

Passing Arguments: Value vs. Reference

Understanding how arguments are passed to subroutines and functions is critical for writing efficient and error-free code. Fortran provides two main ways to pass arguments: **by value** and **by reference**.

Passing by Value

When you pass an argument **by value**, the subroutine or function receives a copy of the argument. Changes made to the argument inside the subroutine or function do not affect the original variable.

```
SUBROUTINE pass_by_value(a)
 INTEGER, INTENT(IN) :: a
 a = 10  ! This change does not affect the original variable
END SUBROUTINE pass_by_value
```

Passing by Reference

When you pass an argument **by reference**, the subroutine or function can modify the original variable. This is more efficient for large data structures like arrays because no copy is made.

```
SUBROUTINE pass_by_reference(a)
 INTEGER, INTENT(INOUT) :: a
 a = 10  ! This change affects the original variable
END SUBROUTINE pass_by_reference
```

- **INTENT(INOUT)** allows the argument to be both read and modified by the subroutine.

Organizing Code with Modules

Fortran allows us to organize our code into **modules**, which are containers for variables, subroutines, and functions. Using modules helps you maintain a clean and modular program structure, making code easier to debug, extend, and reuse.

Defining a Module

A module is defined using the **MODULE** keyword. Here's an example:

```
MODULE math_operations
 CONTAINS
 FUNCTION add_numbers(a, b)
  REAL, INTENT(IN) :: a, b
  REAL :: add_numbers

  add_numbers = a + b
 END FUNCTION add_numbers
END MODULE math_operations
```

This module contains the function **add_numbers**. Once the module is defined, it can be used in any program or subroutine by using the **USE** keyword.

Using a Module

To use the module in a program:

```
PROGRAM test_module
 USE math_operations
 REAL ::result
  result = add_numbers(3.0, 4.5)
 PRINT *, 'The result is:', result
END PROGRAM test_module
```

By organizing related subroutines and functions into modules, you can make your code more manageable and reusable.

To ensure your Fortran programs are efficient, maintainable, and scalable, follow these best practices when using subroutines, functions, and modules.

1. Use Modules for Code Reusability

Organize logically related routines and variables into modules. This encourages code reuse, improves modularity, and makes your program easier to maintain.

2. Pass Arguments by Reference for Large Data Structures

When dealing with large arrays or complex data structures, pass them by reference to avoid unnecessary copying and to enhance performance.

3. Avoid Global Variables

While Fortran allows global variables, it is better to avoid them in modular programming. Instead, pass data explicitly via subroutine or function arguments. This leads to more predictable, less error-prone code.

4. Use the CONTAINS Keyword

In modules, use the **CONTAINS** keyword to include functions or subroutines. This helps maintain a clear structure within the module and reduces the chances of naming conflicts.

Advanced Insights: Performance and Parallelism
Performance Optimization

Fortran's modular design can be highly efficient, but performance optimization is key when working with large data sets or high-performance computing (HPC) applications.

- **Inlining Functions**: For small functions that are called frequently, use the INCLUDE directive or compiler-specific optimization flags to inline the function, reducing the overhead of the function call.

- **Memory Management**: Properly managing memory in modular programs is essential for optimizing performance. Fortran allows explicit memory allocation and deallocation using ALLOCATE and DEALLOCATE, ensuring that memory is efficiently utilized in large-scale problems.

Parallel Computing

In scientific computing and HPC, modular programming is crucial for enabling parallel execution. Fortran 2008 and 2018 introduced enhanced parallel computing features, such as co-arrays and the DO PARALLEL directive. These allow different modules or subroutines to execute concurrently, drastically reducing computation time.

```
! Example of parallelized loop in Fortran 2018
DO PARALLEL I = 1, N
 array(I) = array(I) * 2
END DO
```

By structuring code modularly, you can easily isolate parallelizable sections and make use of modern multi-core processors.

Reflective Questions

- How does modular programming affect the performance of large-scale simulations? What challenges may arise when applying it to parallel computing tasks?

- In what situations would you prefer to pass arguments by reference instead of by value? How does this choice impact memory usage and computation time?

- Consider the trade-offs between code maintainability and performance. How can modularity and performance optimizations coexist in real-world Fortran applications?

Interactive Exercises

Exercise 1:

Write a program that uses a module to store mathematical constants like Pi, Euler's number, and the golden ratio. Then, create a function within the module to calculate the area of a circle using the value of Pi.

Exercise 2:

Design a modular program that computes the determinant of a matrix. Use subroutines for various steps, such as matrix input, calculation of minors, and the final determinant calculation.

Exercise 3:

Implement a parallel program that calculates the sum of the squares of an array of numbers using the **DO PARALLEL** directive in Fortran 2018. Experiment with different array sizes to observe performance gains.

Key Takeaways

- **Modularity** is a key aspect of Fortran programming, enabling code reuse, readability, and maintainability.

- **Subroutines** do not return values, whereas **functions** return a value and can be used directly in expressions.

- **Modules** organize related routines and data, ensuring better code structure and avoiding global variables.

- For performance optimization, pass large data structures by reference and consider parallel programming techniques when scaling up computations.

CHAPTER 6
File Handling in Fortran

In modern computing, data is essential for scientific computation, modeling, and analysis. Handling this data effectively can make or break a simulation or algorithm. Fortran, being one of the most established languages for scientific computing, offers robust mechanisms for managing input and output (I/O), including reading and writing to files. This chapter will explore the foundational aspects of file handling in Fortran, from basic I/O to advanced file access techniques. We will also examine real-world case studies, including handling weather data, to demonstrate how Fortran can be utilized for managing large datasets.

1. Foundations of File Handling in Fortran

Fortran provides several ways to work with files. This section will introduce basic I/O operations, which include reading from and writing to files, as well as explaining the different file access methods available.

1.1 Reading and Writing Data from Files

In Fortran, you can read and write data using the OPEN, READ, and WRITE statements.

Writing to Files:

To write data to a file in Fortran, the following steps are used:

```
PROGRAM WriteToFile
  IMPLICIT NONE
  INTEGER :: unit
  REAL :: temperature
  OPEN(unit=unit, FILE="temperature_data.txt", STATUS="REPLACE")
  WRITE(unit,*) "Temperature Data"
```

```
    WRITE(unit,*) 23.5
    CLOSE(unit)
END PROGRAM WriteToFile
```

In this example:

- The **OPEN** statement opens a file named tempera-ture_data.txt for writing.

- The **STATUS="REPLACE"** option ensures that the file is cre-ated or overwritten if it exists.

- The **WRITE** statement writes data to the file, followed by closing the file using the CLOSE statement.

Reading from Files:

To read data from a file, you can use the READ statement:

```
PROGRAM ReadFromFile
   IMPLICIT NONE
   INTEGER :: unit
   REAL :: temperature
   OPEN(unit=unit, FILE="temperature_data.txt", STATUS="OLD")
   READ(unit,*) temperature
   PRINT*, "Temperature Read From File:", temperature
   CLOSE(unit)
END PROGRAM ReadFromFile
```

In this example:

- The **OPEN** statement opens the file in read-only mode **(STATUS="OLD").**

- The **READ** statement reads a real number from the file and stores it in the variable temperature.

- The program then prints the value of temperature.

2. Handling Different File Formats

Fortran supports a variety of file formats, each suited to different use cases. It is important to understand how to deal with different formats such as sequential and direct access files.

2.1 Sequential Access Files

Sequential access files are the most common type of files, where data is written or read in a linear sequence. These files can be processed in a straightforward manner, where each read or write operation occurs one after the other.

Example:

```
PROGRAM SequentialAccess
  IMPLICIT NONE
  INTEGER :: unit, i
  REAL :: value
  OPEN(unit=unit, FILE="data.txt", STATUS="REPLACE")
  DO i = 1, 5
     WRITE(unit,*) i, 1.0 * i
  END DO
  CLOSE(unit)
END PROGRAM SequentialAccess
```

This program writes five pairs of integers and their corresponding floating-point values into a sequential file data.txt.

2.2 Direct Access Files

For direct access files, Fortran allows you to read and write data at specific record positions, providing greater flexibility, especially when dealing with large datasets.

Example:

```
PROGRAM DirectAccess
  IMPLICIT NONE
  INTEGER :: unit, recNum
  REAL :: value
```

```
    OPEN(unit=unit, FILE="direct_access.dat", STATUS="REPLACE", ACCESS="DIRECT",
RECL=4)
    DO recNum = 1, 5
        value = 1.0 * recNum
        WRITE(unit, REC=recNum) value
    END DO
    CLOSE(unit)
END PROGRAM DirectAccess
```

This program writes five records to the file direct_access.dat and can be read in any order using the REC specifier.

3. Case Study: Handling Weather Data with Fortran

In the real world, handling large datasets is a common requirement. Weather data is a prime example, with massive datasets containing temperature, pressure, and wind speed readings.

3.1 Problem Statement

Given a large dataset of weather data, we need to:

- Read multiple years of data from a file.

- Process it to compute daily average temperatures.

- Write the processed data to another file.

3.2 Solution Approach

```
PROGRAM WeatherDataProcessing
    IMPLICIT NONE
    INTEGER :: i, unit_in, unit_out, numRecords
    REAL :: temperature, dailyAvgTemp, totalTemp
    CHARACTER(LEN=20) :: date

    OPEN(unit=unit_in, FILE="weather_data.csv", STATUS="OLD")
    OPEN(unit=unit_out, FILE="processed_weather_data.txt", STATUS="REPLACE")

    totalTemp = 0.0
    numRecords = 0

    DO
        READ(unit_in,*, IOSTAT=i) date, temperature
```

```
    IF (i /= 0) EXIT
    totalTemp = totalTemp + temperature
    numRecords = numRecords + 1
  END DO

  dailyAvgTemp = totalTemp / numRecords
  WRITE(unit_out,*) "Daily Average Temperature: ", dailyAvgTemp
  CLOSE(unit_in)
  CLOSE(unit_out)
END PROGRAM WeatherDataProcessing
```

In this case:

- The program opens the file weather_data.csv for reading and processes each record in a loop.

- It calculates the average temperature and writes the result to processed_weather_data.txt.

- The IOSTAT parameter is used to check for the end of the file.

4. Best Practices for Modular Programming with File Handling

When working with file I/O in Fortran, it is essential to maintain code modularity, efficiency, and clarity. Below are some key best practices.

4.1 Use of Subroutines and Functions

Breaking down tasks into subroutines and functions can make the code more organized and reusable. Here's an example of using subroutines to handle file reading and writing:

```
SUBROUTINE WriteData(unit, data)
  INTEGER, INTENT(IN) :: unit
  REAL, INTENT(IN) :: data
  WRITE(unit,*) data
END SUBROUTINE WriteData
```

```
SUBROUTINE ReadData(unit, data)
   INTEGER, INTENT(IN) :: unit
   REAL, INTENT(OUT) :: data
   READ(unit,*) data
END SUBROUTINE ReadData
```

4.2 Error Handling and File Closing

Always check the status of file operations. Use the IOSTAT specifier to catch errors during reading and writing, and ensure that files are properly closed.

```
INTEGER :: i
OPEN(unit=unit, FILE="data.txt", STATUS="OLD", IOSTAT=i)
IF (i /= 0) THEN
   PRINT*, "Error opening file"
   STOP
END IF
```

Reflective Questions

1. How can file handling be optimized when dealing with very large datasets (e.g., multi-terabyte weather data)?

2. What are the advantages and disadvantages of sequential access files vs. direct access files in terms of speed and memory usage?

3. How can Fortran's file handling be leveraged in high-performance computing (HPC) applications, especially when working with distributed systems?

Interactive Exercises

Exercise 1: Write a Fortran program that reads a list of student names and their grades from a file. It should then compute the average grade and write the result to another file.

Exercise 2: Modify the weather data processing program to compute the highest and lowest temperatures for each month, and then output the results to a new file.

Exercise 3: Implement a Fortran program that uses direct access files to store and retrieve large matrices of numerical data. Implement error checking to ensure that the data is correctly written and read from the file.

Key Takeaways

- **File Handling:** Fortran provides powerful file handling features, including sequential and direct access file types.

- **Best Practices:** Use subroutines and error handling to write clean, efficient code for reading and writing files.

- **Real-World Applications:** File handling in Fortran is widely used in fields such as climate modeling, engineering, and scientific simulations.

- **Advanced Insights:** Use performance optimizations such as buffered I/O and parallel computing when dealing with large datasets.

CHAPTER 7
Advanced Features of Fortran

Fortran has long been the workhorse of scientific computing. While its early versions were designed for procedural programming, modern Fortran introduces powerful features that allow developers to tackle complex computational problems with flexibility, efficiency, and clarity. This chapter explores **advanced features of Fortran**, including dynamic memory allocation, pointers, user-defined data types, and custom operator overloading.

By the end of this chapter, you'll not only master these features but also understand how they empower developers to write cleaner, more modular, and performance-optimized code. Each concept will be reinforced through practical exercises, real-world applications, and rare insights into how these features are leveraged in cutting-edge research and industry.

7.1 Dynamic Memory Allocation
What is Dynamic Memory Allocation?

Dynamic memory allocation allows programs to manage memory more flexibly, particularly for scenarios where the required memory size is not known at compile time. This is especially useful in scientific applications dealing with large datasets or simulations.

In Fortran, dynamic memory is allocated using **allocatable arrays** or the **ALLOCATE/DEALLOCATE** constructs.

Example 7.1: Allocatable Arrays

```fortran
PROGRAM dynamic_memory
 IMPLICIT NONE
 INTEGER, ALLOCATABLE :: numbers(:)
 INTEGER :: n, i

 ! Ask the user for the size of the array
 PRINT *, "Enter the number of elements:"
 READ(*, *) n

 ! Dynamically allocate memory for the array
 ALLOCATE(numbers(n))
 PRINT *, "Memory allocated for", n, "elements."

 ! Populate and print the array
 DO i = 1, n
   numbers(i) = i * 2
 END DO
 PRINT *, "Array contents: ", numbers

 ! Deallocate the memory
 DEALLOCATE(numbers)
 PRINT *, "Memory deallocated."
END PROGRAM dynamic_memory
```

Common Pitfalls and Solutions

- **Failure to Deallocate Memory**: Not deallocating memory can lead to memory leaks. Always use the DEALLOCATE statement when memory is no longer needed.

- **Attempting to Access Unallocated Arrays**: Ensure that an array is allocated before using it. Use the ALLOCATED intrinsic function to check:

```fortran
IF (.NOT. ALLOCATED(numbers)) THEN
  PRINT *, "Array not allocated!"
END IF
```

7.2 Pointers: Understanding and Utilizing

Pointers in Fortran allow variables to reference memory locations directly, enabling flexible data structures like linked lists or matrices with irregular shapes. Unlike allocatable arrays, pointers can be reassigned to point to different targets during program execution.

Declaring Pointers

Pointers are declared with the POINTER attribute. To use a pointer, its target must first be allocated or assigned.

```
INTEGER, POINTER :: ptr(:)
INTEGER, TARGET :: target_array(10)
```

The **TARGET** attribute identifies variables that a pointer can reference.

Example 7.2: Using Pointers with Arrays

```
PROGRAM pointer_example
  IMPLICIT NONE
  INTEGER, POINTER :: ptr(:)
  INTEGER, TARGET :: array(5)
  INTEGER :: i

  ! Initialize the target array
  array = (/1, 2, 3, 4, 5/)

  ! Associate the pointer with the target
  ptr => array

  ! Modify the array through the pointer
  DO i = 1, 5
    ptr(i) = ptr(i) * 2
  END DO

  PRINT *, "Modified array:", array
END PROGRAM pointer_example
```

Advanced Usage of Pointers

Pointers are essential for creating advanced data structures like linked lists. They are also useful in scenarios where dynamic real-location of memory is required during runtime.

Debugging Pointer Errors

- **Dangling Pointers**: Accessing a pointer after its target has been deallocated leads to undefined behavior. Use **ASSOCIATED** to verify pointer validity:

```
IF (.NOT. ASSOCIATED(ptr)) THEN
   PRINT *, "Pointer is not associated with any target."
END IF
```

7.3 User-Defined Types (Derived Data Types)

Derived data types allow you to group related variables into a single structure, making your programs more modular and easier to maintain. This feature is especially useful for applications involving complex data, such as simulations or data analysis.

Defining a Derived Data Type

```
TYPE :: WeatherData
  REAL :: temperature
  REAL :: humidity
  REAL :: wind_speed
END TYPE WeatherData
```

Example 7.3: Using User-Defined Types

```
PROGRAM weather_analysis
  IMPLICIT NONE
  TYPE(WeatherData) :: today
  today%temperature = 30.5
  today%humidity = 70.0
```

```
  today%wind_speed = 15.0

  PRINT *, "Today's Weather:"
  PRINT *, "Temperature:", today%temperature
  PRINT *, "Humidity:", today%humidity
  PRINT *, "Wind Speed:", today%wind_speed
END PROGRAM weather_analysis
```

7.4 Operator Overloading and Custom Operators

Fortran allows developers to define custom operators for user-defined types, enabling intuitive mathematical expressions for complex data structures.

Example 7.4: Overloading the Addition Operator

```
MODULE operator_overloading
  IMPLICIT NONE
  TYPE :: ComplexNumber
    REAL :: real_part
    REAL :: imaginary_part
  END TYPE ComplexNumber

  INTERFACE OPERATOR(+)
    MODULE PROCEDURE add_complex
  END INTERFACE

CONTAINS
  FUNCTION add_complex(a, b) RESULT(sum)
    TYPE(ComplexNumber), INTENT(IN) :: a, b
    TYPE(ComplexNumber) :: sum
    sum%real_part = a%real_part + b%real_part
    sum%imaginary_part = a%imaginary_part + b%imaginary_part
  END FUNCTION add_complex
END MODULE operator_overloading

PROGRAM test_operators
  USE operator_overloading
  IMPLICIT NONE
  TYPE(ComplexNumber) :: c1, c2, result
```

```
! Assign values
c1 = ComplexNumber(2.0, 3.0)
c2 = ComplexNumber(1.0, 4.0)

! Use the overloaded operator
result = c1 + c2
PRINT *, "Sum: ", result%real_part, "+", result%imaginary_part, "i"
END PROGRAM test_operators
```

Reflective Questions

1. How does Fortran's approach to dynamic memory management compare to other languages like C++ or Python?

2. How can pointers enhance flexibility in simulations or data processing workflows?

3. What are the performance trade-offs of using derived data types and operator overloading in high-performance computing?

Interactive Exercises

1. **Dynamic Memory Allocation**: Write a program that dynamically allocates a matrix based on user input and calculates its transpose.

2. **Pointers**: Implement a linked list in Fortran using pointers.

3. **User-Defined Types**: Create a program to manage a library's book records using derived data types.

4. **Operator Overloading**: Define custom operators to perform vector addition and scalar multiplication for a user-defined Vector type.

Key Takeaways

- **Dynamic Memory**: Mastery of ALLOCATE and DEALLO-CATE empowers you to handle large and unpredictable datasets efficiently.

- **Pointers**: Essential for advanced data structures and memory management.

- **Derived Types**: Enable cleaner, modular code for complex data relationships.

- **Custom Operators**: Enhance code readability and make operations on user-defined types more intuitive.

CHAPTER 8
Error Handling and Debugging in Fortran

In any programming journey, errors and debugging are inevitable. Fortran, despite its reliability in scientific computing, is no exception. From simple syntax errors to complex runtime issues, understanding how to effectively handle errors and debug your code is crucial for developing robust applications. This chapter equips you with the tools, techniques, and best practices needed to identify, troubleshoot, and fix errors in Fortran programs.

By exploring common compilation errors, debugging tools, defensive coding strategies, and advanced error-trapping techniques, this chapter aims to make you proficient at building reliable and fault-tolerant Fortran applications. Whether you're a beginner learning the basics or a seasoned developer looking for advanced insights, this chapter has something for everyone.

Common Compilation Errors and Fixes

8.1.1 Syntax Errors

Syntax errors are among the most common issues encountered when writing Fortran code. They occur when the compiler detects code that does not conform to the language's grammar.

Examples and Fixes

1. **Missing END Statement**

```
PROGRAM missing_end
  PRINT *, "Hello, World!"
! Missing END statement here
```

Fix: Add the **END** statement.

```
PROGRAM missing_end
  PRINT *, "Hello, World!"
END PROGRAM missing_end
```

2. Mismatched Parentheses

```
PRINT *, (3 + 2
```

Fix: Ensure all parentheses are correctly matched.

```
PRINT *, (3 + 2)
```

3. Incorrect Variable Declaration

```
REAL :: x
x = "String Value" ! Error: Type mismatch
```

Fix: Assign variables matching their type.

```
REAL :: x
x = 3.14
```

8.1.2 Logical Errors

Logical errors do not prevent the program from running but cause it to produce incorrect results. For example, an off-by-one error in a loop can lead to miscalculations.

Example

```
DO i = 1, 10
  PRINT *, i * 2
END DO
```

If the intention is to calculate odd numbers, the logic is flawed.

Fix:

```
DO i = 1, 10
  PRINT *, i * 2 - 1
END DO
```

8.1.3 Runtime Errors

These errors occur during the execution of a program and often stem from invalid operations, such as division by zero or accessing out-of-bounds array elements.

Example

```
PROGRAM runtime_error
  INTEGER :: x, y
  x = 10
  y = 0
  PRINT *, x / y ! Division by zero
END PROGRAM runtime_error
```

Fix: Add a conditional check.

```
IF (y /= 0) THEN
  PRINT *, x / y
ELSE
  PRINT *, "Error: Division by zero"
END IF
```

8.2 Debugging Tools and Techniques

Debugging is the process of identifying and fixing errors in a program. Effective debugging requires both tools and strategies.

8.2.1 Compiler Options for Debugging

Most Fortran compilers provide debugging flags to identify errors during compilation.

1. **Enabling Debugging Information** Use the -g flag (for GNU Fortran):

```
gfortran -g program.f90 -o program
```

This enables debugging information for use with debugging tools like gdb.

2. **Enabling Warning Messages** Use the -Wall flag to display all warnings:

```
gfortran -Wall program.f90 -o program
```

3. **Enabling Array Bound Checks** Use the -fcheck=bounds option to detect out-of-bounds array access:

```
gfortran -fcheck=bounds program.f90 -o program
```

8.2.2 Debugging with Tools

1. **GNU Debugger (gdb)**

   o **Start a Debugging Session**:

```
gdb ./program
```

   o **Set Breakpoints**:

```
break main
```

   o **Run the Program**:

```
run
```

   o **Inspect Variables**:

```
print variable_name
```

2. **IDE Debuggers** Modern IDEs like Visual Studio Code or Code::Blocks provide graphical interfaces for debugging Fortran programs, making it easier to set breakpoints, inspect variables, and step through code.

3. **Profilers** Tools like gprof help identify performance bottlenecks in addition to runtime errors.

8.2.3 Debugging Strategies

1. **Print Statements** Insert print statements to display variable values at different stages of execution.

```
PRINT *, "Value of x: ", x
```

1. **Divide and Conquer** Break the program into smaller parts and test each part independently to isolate the source of errors.

2. **Rubber Duck Debugging** Explain your code to someone (or something) else to identify logical inconsistencies.

8.3 Writing Defensive Code with Error Trapping

Defensive coding involves anticipating potential errors and handling them gracefully to ensure program reliability.

8.3.1 Error Handling with Status Codes

Use the IOMSG and IOSTAT specifiers in I/O operations to detect and handle errors.

Example

```
PROGRAM defensive_code
 INTEGER :: io_status
 OPEN(UNIT=10, FILE="data.txt", STATUS="OLD", IOSTAT=io_status)

 IF (io_status /= 0) THEN
   PRINT *, "Error opening file."
 ELSE
   PRINT *, "File opened successfully."
 END IF
END PROGRAM defensive_code
```

8.3.2 Assert Statements

Fortran does not have built-in assertions, but you can create your own:

```fortran
SUBROUTINE assert(condition, message)
  LOGICAL, INTENT(IN) :: condition
  CHARACTER(*), INTENT(IN) :: message
  IF (.NOT. condition) THEN
    PRINT *, "Assertion failed: ", message
    STOP
  END IF
END SUBROUTINE assert
```

8.4 Best Practices for Reliable Code

1. **Follow a Consistent Coding Style**

   o Use meaningful variable names.

   o Indent code blocks for readability.

2. **Use Modular Programming**

   o Break large programs into smaller subroutines and modules.

3. **Perform Rigorous Testing**

   o Test edge cases, such as empty inputs or extreme values.

4. **Document Your Code**

   o Include comments to explain complex logic.

5. **Adopt Version Control**

   o Use tools like Git to track changes and collaborate effectively.

8.5 Real-World Debugging Scenario

Case Study: Debugging a Climate Simulation Model

A climate simulation program was producing incorrect temperature projections. The error stemmed from:

1. **An off-by-one error in a loop**: The loop iterated one element too far, leading to an invalid array index.

2. **Improper handling of missing data**: Missing temperature data caused runtime crashes.

Steps to Fix

1. **Enabled Array Bound Checks**: This revealed the out-of-bounds array access.

2. **Added Conditional Checks**: Ensured missing data was replaced with default values.

3. **Tested with Debugging Tools**: Used gdb to step through the program and verify correctness.

Interactive Exercises

1. **Error Handling**: Write a program to read numbers from a file and calculate their average. Include error handling for:

    o Missing files

    o Invalid data

    o Division by zero

2. **Debugging Challenge**: Debug the following program, which should calculate the factorial of a number but contains errors:

```
PROGRAM factorial
 INTEGER :: i, num, fact
 READ(*, *) num
 fact = 0
 DO i = 1, num
  fact = fact * i
 END DO
 PRINT *, "Factorial:", fact
END PROGRAM factorial
```

3. **Defensive Coding**: Modify the Fibonacci series program to handle invalid user input (e.g., negative numbers).

Key Takeaways

- Understanding and addressing errors is essential for writing reliable and robust Fortran programs.

- Debugging tools and strategies, such as gdb, compiler flags, and print statements, streamline the error resolution process.

- Writing defensive code ensures that programs handle unexpected situations gracefully.

- Best practices like modular programming, rigorous testing, and clear documentation minimize the risk of errors and simplify debugging.

CHAPTER 9
High-Performance Computing with Fortran

High-performance computing (HPC) has revolutionized industries like climate modeling, fluid dynamics, and large-scale scientific simulations. As one of the oldest and most trusted programming languages in scientific computing, **Fortran** continues to play a vital role in delivering unparalleled computational performance. This chapter will provide a comprehensive guide to using Fortran in HPC, covering parallel programming, coarrays, multithreading with OpenMP, and optimization techniques for achieving exceptional speed and efficiency.

For beginners, this chapter serves as a foundation for understanding Fortran's capabilities in parallel and distributed computing. For advanced users, it offers cutting-edge insights, tips, and rarely discussed techniques that are critical in modern HPC scenarios.

9.1 Introduction to Parallel Programming

Parallel programming involves dividing computational tasks into smaller, independent units that can run simultaneously across multiple processors. Fortran excels in this space because of its intrinsic features, such as coarrays and its compatibility with external parallel programming models like OpenMP and MPI.

9.1.1 Why Parallel Programming?

- **Performance**: Reduces execution time by leveraging multi-core processors.

- **Scalability**: Enables handling of massive datasets across distributed systems.

- **Relevance in Scientific Applications**: Essential in climate simulations, fluid dynamics, and molecular modeling.

9.1.2 Key Concepts in Parallel Programming

- **Task Parallelism**: Independent tasks execute concurrently.

- **Data Parallelism**: Data is divided among processors, with each performing the same operation.

- **Synchronization**: Ensures processors communicate and coordinate properly.

9.1.3 The Fortran Advantage in HPC

Fortran's design emphasizes:

- Simplicity in array operations (essential for data parallelism).

- Features like coarrays for distributed memory systems.

- Compatibility with HPC tools like OpenMP and MPI.

9.2 Coarrays: Fortran's Parallelism Features

9.2.1 What Are Coarrays?

Introduced in Fortran 2008, coarrays enable **partitioned global address space (PGAS)** programming. This allows multiple images (independent execution units) to communicate and work on shared data efficiently.

9.2.2 Syntax and Structure

Coarrays extend Fortran's array concept with an additional set of dimensions for distributed memory.

Basic Syntax

```
REAL :: array1[*]   ! Declares a coarray shared across all images
INTEGER :: array2[5] ! Declares a coarray with 5 images
```

Key Operations

- **Accessing Data on Another Image**:

```
array1[2] = 42.0  ! Assigns 42.0 to array1 on image 2
```

- **Synchronization**:

```
SYNC ALL       ! Ensures all images reach the same execution point
```

- **Local and Remote Memory**:

```
x = array2[3]    ! Fetch data from array2 on image 3
```

9.2.3 Example: Distributed Matrix Addition

```
PROGRAM matrix_addition
  REAL, DIMENSION(100,100) :: A[*], B[*], C[*]
  INTEGER :: i, j

  ! Initialize matrices
  A = 1.0
  B = 2.0

  ! Perform matrix addition in parallel
  C = A + B

  ! Synchronize all images
  SYNC ALL
  IF (THIS_IMAGE() == 1) THEN
    PRINT *, "Result on Image 1:", C
  END IF
END PROGRAM matrix_addition
```

9.3 Integrating OpenMP for Multithreading

9.3.1 What is OpenMP?

OpenMP is a standard API for shared-memory parallelism that enables multithreading in Fortran. It simplifies the division of computational tasks across multiple CPU cores.

9.3.2 Basics of OpenMP

To use OpenMP:

1. Include the OpenMP module:

```
USE OMP_LIB
```

2. Compile with OpenMP support:

```
gfortran -fopenmp program.f90 -o program
```

9.3.3 Parallel Constructs

- **Parallel Region**:

```
!$OMP PARALLEL
  PRINT *, "This is thread ", OMP_GET_THREAD_NUM()
!$OMP END PARALLEL
```

- **Parallelizing Loops**:

```
!$OMP PARALLEL DO
DO i = 1, 1000
  array(i) = i * 2
END DO
!$OMP END PARALLEL DO
```

9.3.4 Advanced OpenMP Techniques

1. **Thread Synchronization**:

```
!$OMP CRITICAL
  sum = sum + value
!$OMP END CRITICAL
```

2. **Dynamic Scheduling**:

```
!$OMP DO SCHEDULE(DYNAMIC)
```

9.4 Optimizing Code for Speed and Efficiency

Optimization ensures that code runs faster while consuming fewer resources. Fortran's design facilitates performance, but additional techniques can maximize speed and efficiency.

9.4.1 Array Operations

Leverage Fortran's array syntax for efficient computations.

```
A = B + C   ! Faster than using explicit DO loops
```

9.4.2 Minimize I/O Operations

- Avoid excessive use of WRITE or READ within loops.

- Use buffering to reduce file I/O overhead.

9.4.3 Loop Unrolling

Unroll loops to reduce the overhead of loop control:

```
DO i = 1, N, 2
  A(i) = B(i) + C(i)
  A(i+1) = B(i+1) + C(i+1)
END DO
```

9.4.4 Memory Alignment

Optimize memory layout for efficient cache utilization:

- Use contiguous arrays.

- Align data for vectorized operations.

9.5 Real-World Applications

9.5.1 Climate Modeling

Simulating climate requires massive data processing. Coarrays enable distributed computations, while OpenMP accelerates localized tasks like solving differential equations.

9.5.2 Computational Fluid Dynamics (CFD)

Fortran's array processing and parallelization capabilities make it ideal for CFD simulations in aerodynamics or weather prediction.

9.5.3 Molecular Dynamics

Parallelized Fortran programs can simulate atomic interactions at large scales using coarrays for distributed data and OpenMP for local calculations.

Exercise 1: Coarray Basics

Write a program to calculate the sum of elements in an array using coarrays. Each image should handle a subset of the array, and the results should be combined.

Exercise 2: OpenMP Loop Parallelization

Modify the following code to run in parallel using OpenMP:

```
DO i = 1, 1000
  array(i) = i * 2
END DO
```

Exercise 3: Optimize Matrix Multiplication

Write a Fortran program to perform matrix multiplication. Optimize the program for both single-threaded and multi-threaded execution.

Reflective Questions

1. How does Fortran's coarray feature compare with MPI for distributed memory systems?

2. What are the trade-offs of using OpenMP for multithreading versus coarrays for distributed memory parallelism?

3. How would you optimize a Fortran program for GPU-based computing?

Key Takeaways

- Fortran is a powerful tool for high-performance computing, offering intrinsic parallelism features like coarrays and compatibility with OpenMP.

- Optimizing code for HPC involves efficient array operations, minimizing I/O, and leveraging parallel constructs.

- Real-world applications like climate modeling, CFD, and molecular dynamics showcase Fortran's strength in tackling large-scale computational problems.

CHAPTER 10
Real-World Applications of Fortran

Fortran has remained a cornerstone of scientific and engineering computations for decades. Its design, centered on numerical precision, array manipulation, and high-performance computing, has made it the go-to language for tackling real-world challenges in industries such as climate science, finance, aerospace, and engineering. In this chapter, we will explore how Fortran is used in real-world scenarios, providing case studies and examples that demonstrate its power and versatility.

Introduction

This chapter dives into the practical applications of Fortran, highlighting its critical role in solving complex problems in numerical simulations, computational fluid dynamics (CFD), financial modeling, and more. We will also discuss how custom Fortran libraries are developed for specialized purposes. By the end of this chapter, you will gain insight into how the concepts and tools learned so far translate into actionable solutions for industry challenges.

Why Focus on Real-World Applications?

Fortran is not just a theoretical language—it is embedded in the workflows of industries requiring high-precision calculations and robust performance. From weather forecasting to financial risk analysis, Fortran continues to shine where numerical accuracy, speed, and scalability are paramount.

1. Fortran in Numerical Simulations

Numerical simulations form the backbone of many industries, from physics to biology. Fortran's performance and support for mathematical precision make it ideal for building and running simulations that require immense computational resources.

Case Study: Climate Modeling

Climate modeling is one of the most computationally intensive tasks undertaken today. Models such as the Community Earth System Model (CESM) are powered by Fortran.

Example: Heat Diffusion Simulation

This example demonstrates how Fortran can simulate heat diffusion in a 2D grid over time, using numerical techniques such as the finite difference method (FDM).

```fortran
PROGRAM HeatDiffusion
 IMPLICIT NONE
 INTEGER, PARAMETER :: NX = 100, NY = 100, NSTEPS = 100
 REAL, PARAMETER :: DX = 0.01, DY = 0.01, DT = 0.001, ALPHA = 0.01
 REAL :: temp(NX, NY), temp_new(NX, NY)
 INTEGER :: i, j, step

 ! Initialize temperature grid
 temp = 0.0
 temp(NX/2, NY/2) = 100.0  ! Heat source at the center

 ! Time-stepping loop
 DO step = 1, NSTEPS
  DO i = 2, NX-1
   DO j = 2, NY-1
    temp_new(i, j) = temp(i, j) + ALPHA * DT * &
          ((temp(i+1, j) - 2.0*temp(i, j) + temp(i-1, j)) / DX**2 + &
          (temp(i, j+1) - 2.0*temp(i, j) + temp(i, j-1)) / DY**2)
   END DO
  END DO

  temp = temp_new
 END DO

 PRINT *, "Simulation complete."
END PROGRAM HeatDiffusion
```

Applications

- Predicting global warming trends.

- Simulating the behavior of natural systems like ocean currents.

2. Using Fortran for Computational Fluid Dynamics (CFD)

Fortran's capability to handle large arrays and solve partial differential equations (PDEs) efficiently makes it the perfect candidate for CFD applications. CFD is used to simulate the behavior of fluids, gases, and their interactions with surfaces.

Case Study: Aerospace Engineering

In aerospace engineering, CFD is used to design aerodynamic structures like aircraft wings. The Navier-Stokes equations, which govern fluid motion, are solved numerically using Fortran.

Example: Solving a 2D Euler Equation

A simple numerical solver for 2D fluid flow based on the Euler equations can be implemented in Fortran. While this example uses a simplified model, it demonstrates the core principles.

```fortran
PROGRAM EulerSolver
  IMPLICIT NONE
  INTEGER, PARAMETER :: NX = 100, NY = 100, NSTEPS = 100
  REAL, DIMENSION(NX, NY) :: rho, u, v, e, p  ! Density, velocity, and energy
  REAL, PARAMETER :: DX = 0.01, DY = 0.01, DT = 0.001
  INTEGER :: i, j, step

  ! Initialize flow field
  rho = 1.0
  u = 0.0
  v = 0.0
  e = 1.0
```

```
! Time-stepping loop
DO step = 1, NSTEPS
  ! (Simplified update logic goes here)
END DO

PRINT *, "CFD simulation complete."
END PROGRAM EulerSolver
```

Applications

- Designing vehicles to minimize drag and fuel consumption.

- Predicting the behavior of airflow around buildings.

3. Fortran in Finance and Risk Modeling

Although typically associated with science and engineering, Fortran has also found a niche in financial modeling. Many legacy systems in financial institutions rely on Fortran for risk analysis, derivative pricing, and portfolio optimization.

Case Study: Monte Carlo Simulations in Risk Analysis

Monte Carlo simulations are extensively used to model uncertain outcomes in financial scenarios. Fortran's ability to handle large datasets and its speed make it suitable for implementing these simulations.

Example: Pricing an Option Using Monte Carlo Simulations

This example calculates the price of a European call option using Monte Carlo techniques.

```
PROGRAM MonteCarloOptionPricing
  IMPLICIT NONE
  INTEGER, PARAMETER :: N = 1000000 ! Number of simulations
  REAL, PARAMETER :: S0 = 100.0, K = 100.0, T = 1.0, R = 0.05, SIGMA = 0.2
```

```fortran
REAL :: dt, payoff, sum_payoff, option_price
REAL :: S, Z
INTEGER :: i
CALL RANDOM_SEED()

dt = T
sum_payoff = 0.0

DO i = 1, N
  CALL RANDOM_NUMBER(Z)
  Z = SQRT(-2.0 * LOG(Z)) * COS(2.0 * 3.14159 * Z)  ! Generate random Gaussian
  S = S0 * EXP((R - 0.5 * SIGMA**2) * dt + SIGMA * SQRT(dt) * Z)
  payoff = MAX(0.0, S - K)
  sum_payoff = sum_payoff + payoff
END DO

option_price = EXP(-R * T) * sum_payoff / N
PRINT *, "Option Price: ", option_price
END PROGRAM MonteCarloOptionPricing
```

Applications

- Predicting portfolio risk.

- Pricing complex derivatives.

4. Developing Custom Libraries for Specialized Applications

Custom Fortran libraries enable developers to address specific computational needs that standard libraries may not cover. For example, a research team working on quantum mechanics simulations might develop a library to handle specialized matrix operations.

Best Practices for Developing Libraries

- Use **modules** to organize code and promote reusability.

- Write **unit tests** to ensure the library's reliability.

- Document the API thoroughly for ease of use.

Example: A Linear Algebra Library

Here's a snippet of a custom matrix multiplication subroutine:

```
MODULE LinearAlgebra
 IMPLICIT NONE
CONTAINS
 SUBROUTINE MatrixMultiply(A, B, C, N)
  REAL, DIMENSION(N, N), INTENT(IN) :: A, B
  REAL, DIMENSION(N, N), INTENT(OUT) :: C
  INTEGER :: i, j, k

  C = 0.0
  DO i = 1, N
   DO j = 1, N
    DO k = 1, N
     C(i, j) = C(i, j) + A(i, k) * B(k, j)
    END DO
   END DO
  END DO
 END SUBROUTINE MatrixMultiply
END MODULE LinearAlgebra
```

Applications

- Creating reusable libraries for academic research.

- Streamlining large-scale industrial computations.

Exercises
Beginner

1. Simulate the growth of a population using a simple exponential model.

Intermediate

2. Implement a solver for a 1D wave equation using finite difference methods.

Advanced

3. Create a custom Fortran library for solving large sparse linear systems.

Key Takeaways:
- Fortran excels in handling computationally intensive tasks like numerical simulations and CFD.

- Its speed and precision make it indispensable in industries such as finance and engineering.

- Developing custom libraries can unlock new possibilities for specialized applications.

CHAPTER 11
Interoperability with Other Languages

In today's modern programming landscape, few projects are completed using a single programming language. Scientific computing, engineering applications, and high-performance computing often require leveraging the strengths of multiple programming languages. Fortran, with its unrivaled speed and numerical capabilities, continues to play a critical role as the backbone of many performance-intensive systems. However, when combined with other popular languages like **C/C++**, **Python**, and **MATLAB**, Fortran's true potential can be fully unleashed.

This chapter will guide you through **seamless interoperability** between Fortran and other languages. You will learn how to link Fortran with C/C++, integrate Python for scripting and data analysis, and leverage MATLAB for scientific visualization. These skills allow you to **develop multilingual solutions** that bring together the best of all worlds, enhancing flexibility and modernizing your Fortran-based projects.

1. Linking Fortran with C/C++

Fortran and C/C++ are often used together to balance Fortran's computational power with C/C++'s system-level programming features. Combining these languages allows you to use C/C++ libraries, expand system compatibility, or develop hybrid software solutions.

Why Combine Fortran and C/C++?

- Access low-level system resources via C.

- Leverage existing C/C++ libraries for enhanced functionality.

- Combine Fortran's numerical power with C++'s object-oriented capabilities.

1.1 Understanding the Fortran-C Interoperability Standard

Fortran 2003 introduced the **ISO_C_BINDING** module, which allows Fortran to directly interact with C. This module makes it possible to declare variables and subroutines that are compatible with C's calling conventions.

Basic Syntax: To declare a C-compatible subroutine in Fortran:

```
module c_binding_example
 use, intrinsic :: iso_c_binding
 implicit none

 interface
   subroutine c_function_example(x) bind(C, name="c_function_example")
     use iso_c_binding
     real(c_double), intent(inout) :: x
   end subroutine c_function_example
 end interface
end module c_binding_example
```

Here, **bind(C)** ensures compatibility with C's name mangling system, and **c_double** specifies a double-precision variable.

1.2 Example: Calling a C Function from Fortran

Let's write a simple **C function** that computes the square of a number and call it from a Fortran program.

C Code:

```
#include <stdio.h>

void square_function(double *x) {
    *x = (*x) * (*x);
}
```

Fortran Code:

```
program call_c_example
  use, intrinsic :: iso_c_binding
  implicit none

  interface
    subroutine square_function(x) bind(C, name="square_function")
      use iso_c_binding
      real(c_double), intent(inout) :: x
    end subroutine square_function
  end interface

  real(c_double) :: num
  num = 3.0

  print *, "Original number:", num
  call square_function(num)
  print *, "Squared number:", num
end program call_c_example
```

Steps to Compile and Run:

1. Compile the C code into an object file:

```
gcc -c square_function.c -o square_function.o
```

2. Compile and link the Fortran code with the C object file:

```
gfortran call_c_example.f90 square_function.o -o run_example
```

3. Execute the program:

```
./run_example
```

Output:

```
Original number: 3.0
Squared number: 9.0
```

1.3 Calling Fortran Subroutines from C

The reverse process (calling Fortran from C) is just as straightforward. Use the bind(C) attribute in Fortran to expose subroutines with C-compatible naming.

Fortran Code:

```
subroutine cube_function(x) bind(C, name="cube_function")
  use, intrinsic :: iso_c_binding
  real(c_double), intent(inout) :: x
  x = x * x * x
end subroutine cube_function
```

C Code:

```
#include <stdio.h>

void cube_function(double *x);

int main() {
    double num = 2.0;
    printf("Original number: %f\n", num);
    cube_function(&num);
    printf("Cubed number: %f\n", num);
    return 0;
}
```

Steps to Run: Follow the same compilation and linking process as before.

2. Using Python with Fortran: A Practical Guide

Python's rise in scientific computing is due to its simplicity and powerful libraries like **NumPy**, **Pandas**, and **SciPy**. However, Python's performance for large-scale numerical computations can't match Fortran. By integrating Python with Fortran, you get **ease**

of scripting from Python while retaining Fortran's numerical speed.

2.1 Tools for Integration

- **f2py**: A tool provided by NumPy to wrap Fortran code and make it callable from Python.

- **ctypes/CFFI**: Libraries for interfacing Python with compiled Fortran code.

2.2 Example: Wrapping a Fortran Function with f2py

Suppose you have a Fortran subroutine that computes the dot product of two vectors:

Fortran Code:

```
subroutine dot_product(n, a, b, result)
  integer, intent(in) :: n
  real, intent(in) :: a(n), b(n)
  real, intent(out) :: result
  result = sum(a * b)
end subroutine dot_product
```

Steps to Wrap with f2py:

1. Save the Fortran code in dot_product.f90.

2. Run f2py to create a Python module:

```
f2py -c -m dot_product dot_product.f90
```

3. Use the module in Python:

```
import dot_product
import numpy as np

a = np.array([1.0, 2.0, 3.0], dtype=np.float32)
b = np.array([4.0, 5.0, 6.0], dtype=np.float32)
```

```
result = dot_product.dot_product(len(a), a, b)
print("Dot Product:", result)
```

3. Leveraging Fortran with MATLAB for Scientific Computing

MATLAB is widely used for scientific computing and data visualization. Fortran's computational power can complement MATLAB's interactive environment.

Key Integration Techniques:

- Use **MEX files** to call Fortran routines from MATLAB.

- Export Fortran functions as shared libraries and call them via MATLAB's loadlibrary function.

Reflective Questions

1. Why is **interoperability** critical in modern scientific and engineering applications?

2. How can combining Python's scripting capabilities with Fortran's computational speed optimize workflows?

3. Reflect on scenarios where linking Fortran with C/C++ can be beneficial in large-scale systems.

Interactive Exercises

1. **Exercise 1:** Write a Fortran subroutine that calculates the **element-wise sum** of two arrays and call it from a Python script using f2py.

2. **Exercise 2:** Develop a **C function** that computes the factorial of a number. Call this C function from a Fortran program.

3. **Exercise 3:** Write a **MATLAB MEX file** to call a Fortran subroutine that solves a system of linear equations using LU decomposition.

Key Takeaways

- Fortran's interoperability with **C/C++**, **Python**, and **MATLAB** allows developers to build efficient, multilingual solutions.

- **ISO_C_BINDING** makes Fortran-C integration straightforward and standardized.

- Tools like **f2py** and **MEX files** help seamlessly integrate Fortran with Python and MATLAB for modern scientific workflows.

- Leveraging Fortran's numerical power with other languages maximizes performance and flexibility.

CHAPTER 12
Practical Exercises and Projects

Programming is not just about learning syntax; it's about applying concepts to solve problems and build meaningful projects. In this chapter, you will work on **practical exercises and projects** that will reinforce the knowledge gained throughout this book. These exercises are designed to help you transition from simply understanding Fortran concepts to **applying them effectively** in real-world scenarios.

Whether you are a beginner writing your first program, an intermediate programmer tackling data analysis or solving differential equations, or an advanced user diving into parallel processing and library development, this chapter has something for everyone.

1. Beginner Exercises: Writing Simple Programs
For those just starting with Fortran, these exercises will focus on writing and running simple programs to solidify your understanding of Fortran syntax and core concepts.

Exercise 1.1: Hello, World! Write a Fortran program that prints "Hello, World!" to the screen.

Goal: Familiarize yourself with the structure of a basic Fortran program, including program, end program, and print statements.

Exercise 1.2: Calculating the Sum of Numbers Write a program that prompts the user for two numbers and calculates their sum.

Key Concepts:

- Input/output using read and print.

- Simple arithmetic operations.

Sample Output:

```
Enter first number: 10
Enter second number: 25
The sum is: 35
```

Exercise 1.3: Temperature Conversion Write a program that converts temperatures from Fahrenheit to Celsius using the formula:

$$\text{Celsius} = \tfrac{5}{9}(\text{Fahrenheit} - 32)$$

Challenges for Practice:

- Add error-checking to ensure valid numeric input.

- Enhance the program to convert Celsius back to Fahrenheit.

2. Intermediate Projects

These projects will involve working with arrays, file handling, and numerical algorithms to solve slightly more complex problems.

Project 2.1: Data Analysis with Fortran

Write a program to read a dataset (stored in a text file) of student scores, calculate the average score, and find the highest and lowest scores.

Steps:

1. Create a text file, scores.txt, with a list of numeric scores, one per line.

2. Write a Fortran program to:

   ○ Read the scores into an array.

   ○ Calculate the average score.

   ○ Determine the highest and lowest scores.

Sample Output:

```
Average score: 72.3
Highest score: 98
Lowest score: 45
```

Project 2.2: Solving Differential Equations

Implement Euler's method to solve a first-order ordinary differential equation (ODE):

$$\frac{dy}{dx} = -2y, \ y(0) = 1$$

Steps:

1. Define the differential equation.

2. Use a loop to calculate the solution for discrete values of xxx using the formula:

$$y_{n+1} = y_n + h \cdot f(x_n, y_n)$$

Where **h** is the step size.

Sample Output: Print the values of xxx and yyy at each step.

Challenges for Practice:

- Extend the program to solve higher-order ODEs.

- Implement Runge-Kutta methods for improved accuracy.

3. Advanced Challenges

For experienced programmers, these challenges involve parallel processing and creating reusable code libraries to push the boundaries of your Fortran expertise.

Challenge 3.1: Parallel Processing with Coarrays

Write a Fortran program that uses **coarrays** to calculate the sum of a large array in parallel.

Steps:

1. Create a large array of random numbers.

2. Divide the array into sections, and assign each section to a separate Fortran image.

3. Use coarrays to calculate the partial sum on each image and gather the results to compute the total sum.

Key Concepts:

- Setting up coarrays using codimension.

- Communication between images using intrinsic functions like sync all and this_image.

Expected Output:

The total sum of the array, calculated faster than using a single-threaded approach.

Challenge 3.2: Developing a Fortran Library

Develop a reusable Fortran library that includes:

- Functions for matrix operations (e.g., multiplication, transposition).

- Solvers for linear systems using LU decomposition.

- Numerical differentiation and integration routines.

Steps:

1. Structure your code using modules.

2. Write unit tests to validate each function.

3. Provide documentation and example programs demonstrating how to use the library.

Advanced Goal: Package the library for distribution, making it usable in other projects.

Reflective Questions

1. How does working on practical projects enhance your understanding of Fortran?

2. What challenges did you encounter in applying Fortran to real-world problems, and how did you overcome them?

3. Reflect on how parallel processing with coarrays can improve the performance of computationally intensive tasks.

Interactive Exercises

1. **Exercise 1:** Modify the temperature conversion program (Exercise 1.3) to process a batch of temperatures stored in a file and output the results to a new file.

2. **Exercise 2:** Extend Project 2.1 (Data Analysis) to include additional statistics, such as the median and standard deviation.

3. **Exercise 3:** Create a modular program where one module performs matrix operations, another handles I/O, and the main program uses these modules to solve a matrix equation.

Key Takeaways

- Practical exercises and projects provide hands-on experience, helping you apply Fortran concepts to real-world scenarios.

- Beginner exercises focus on building confidence, while intermediate and advanced challenges push your skills to the next level.

- Advanced tasks like parallel processing and library development prepare you for industry-standard applications of Fortran.

CHAPTER 13
Fortran Best Practices

Programming is not only about solving problems but also about writing code that is clean, maintainable, and easy to understand by others (and by yourself later on!). Best practices are essential for producing high-quality code that stands the test of time, especially in collaborative or long-term projects.

This chapter will cover **best practices for writing clean and professional Fortran code**, from commenting and documentation to leveraging open-source libraries and version control. By adopting these practices, you can elevate the quality of your work and succeed in **real-world Fortran projects**.

1. Writing Clean and Readable Code
Good coding practices help ensure that your programs are easy to understand, debug, and maintain. Here are some essential tips:

1.1. Use Descriptive Variable and Function Names
Avoid cryptic names like X or A1. Use names that clearly describe their purpose, such as temperature, velocity, or calculate_area.

Example: Poor Naming

```
real :: x
x = y + z
```

Example: Good Naming

```
real :: length, width, area
area = length * width
```

1.2. Follow Consistent Indentation and Formatting

Consistently indent loops, conditional blocks, and subprograms to make the program's structure easy to follow.

Example: Indented Code

```
do i = 1, 10
    if (mod(i, 2) == 0) then
        print *, "Even number: ", i
    else
        print *, "Odd number: ", i
    end if
end do
```

1.3. Limit Line Length

Keep lines to a maximum of 80 characters to ensure readability, especially for printed code or when working with older editors.

1.4. Avoid Hard-Coding Constants

Define constants using parameter instead of scattering raw numbers throughout your code.

Example:

```
integer, parameter :: max_iterations = 100
do i = 1, max_iterations
    ! Loop logic here
end do
```

2. Commenting and Documentation Guidelines

Well-documented code is invaluable, especially for collaborative work or revisiting your own code months or years later.

2.1. Comment Regularly and Meaningfully

Write comments to explain *why* a piece of code exists, not just *what* it does.

Example: Poor Comment

```
! This is a loop
do i = 1, n
    a(i) = b(i) + c(i)
end do
```

Example: Good Comment

```
! Compute the element-wise sum of vectors b and c, storing the result in a.
do i = 1, n
    a(i) = b(i) + c(i)
end do
```

2.2. Document Subprograms

For every function or subroutine, include comments at the beginning describing:

- Its purpose

- Input and output variables

- Any assumptions or constraints

Example:

```
!-------------------------------------------------
! Function: calculate_area
! Purpose: Compute the area of a rectangle.
! Inputs: length (real), width (real)
! Outputs: area (real)
!-------------------------------------------------
function calculate_area(length, width)
    real, intent(in) :: length, width
    real :: calculate_area
    calculate_area = length * width
end function calculate_area
```

2.3. Use In-Code Documentation Tools

Explore tools like **FORD (Fortran Documentation Generator)** to create user-friendly documentation directly from your code comments.

3. Version Control for Fortran Projects

Version control is critical for managing changes in your codebase and collaborating with others. Git is the most popular tool for this purpose.

3.1. Why Use Version Control?

- Track changes and revert to previous versions if needed.

- Collaborate efficiently with other developers.

- Maintain backups of your codebase.

3.2. Essential Git Commands for Fortran Developers

- **Initialize a Git Repository**: git init

- **Track Changes**: git add filename

- **Commit Changes**: git commit -m "Description of changes"

- **View History**: git log

- **Work with Remote Repositories**: git push and git pull

3.3. Using .gitignore for Fortran Projects

Ignore unnecessary files (e.g., object files, executables) to keep your repository clean.

Example .gitignore:

```
*.o
*.mod
*.exe
```

4. Leveraging Open-Source Fortran Libraries

Take advantage of open-source Fortran libraries to avoid reinventing the wheel and to speed up development. Here's how:

4.1. Why Use Open-Source Libraries?

- Save time by reusing tested and optimized code.

- Leverage advanced algorithms and utilities.

- Focus on solving your unique problems instead of writing low-level routines.

4.2. Popular Open-Source Fortran Libraries

- **LAPACK**: Linear Algebra routines (e.g., solving systems of equations, eigenvalues).

- **FFTW**: Fast Fourier Transform library for signal processing.

- **NetCDF**: Handling large scientific datasets.

- **HDF5**: Hierarchical data format for large-scale data storage and retrieval.

4.3. Integrating Libraries into Your Fortran Projects

1. Read the library documentation to understand the functionality.

2. Link the library during compilation. For example:

```
gfortran myprogram.f90 -llapack -lblas
```

Reflective Questions

1. Why is writing clean and maintainable code crucial for long-term projects and collaborations?

2. How do commenting and documentation improve your own productivity as well as that of your team?

3. Reflect on how version control and leveraging open-source libraries can streamline your workflow and development process.

Interactive Exercises

1. **Exercise 1:** Refactor a messy Fortran program to make it clean and readable by applying the principles in this chapter.

2. **Exercise 2:** Write a small program and use Git to version-control your changes. Commit every significant modification and view the commit history.

3. **Exercise 3:** Incorporate an open-source library (e.g., LAPACK) into a Fortran program to solve a system of linear equations.

Key Takeaways

- Writing clean and well-documented code ensures better maintainability and collaboration.

- Using tools like Git for version control and leveraging open-source libraries can significantly boost productivity.

- Professional coding practices not only improve your technical skills but also make you a more effective team player.

CHAPTER 14
Future Opportunities with Fortran

As you near the end of your Fortran journey, it's time to look ahead. Mastering Fortran is more than learning syntax and techniques—it's about opening doors to exciting career opportunities, groundbreaking research, and innovative scientific advancements. In this chapter, we'll explore how Fortran can propel your career in **high-performance computing (HPC)**, connect you with research opportunities, and guide you toward resources to stay updated in this evolving field.

Whether you aspire to be a leader in computational science, a contributor to scientific advancements, or simply want to leverage Fortran in your projects, this chapter will show you the way forward.

1. Career Paths in High-Performance Computing (HPC)

Fortran remains a cornerstone of **HPC**, thanks to its efficiency, numerical precision, and performance. Professionals proficient in Fortran are in demand across various domains. Here are some career paths to consider:

1.1. Computational Scientist/Engineer

- Work in academia, industry, or research organizations to solve complex scientific problems.

- Use Fortran for **simulations**, such as weather modeling, computational fluid dynamics (CFD), or astrophysical simulations.

1.2. HPC Software Developer

- Design and optimize software for supercomputers using Fortran.

- Collaborate with scientists to create efficient algorithms for large-scale problems.

1.3. Data Scientist in Scientific Domains

- Analyze large datasets in fields like climatology, genomics, or seismology.

- Combine Fortran's numerical power with modern tools like Python for hybrid workflows.

1.4. Financial Modeler

- Develop quantitative models for risk analysis, derivatives pricing, and market simulations using Fortran's precision for numerical calculations.

2. Research Opportunities in Science and Engineering

Fortran continues to dominate fields that demand high accuracy and performance in numerical computations. Mastery of Fortran opens doors to **cutting-edge research**:

2.1. Climate Science and Meteorology

- Contribute to global climate models or weather forecasting systems like **WRF** (Weather Research and Forecasting).

2.2. Physics and Chemistry

- Simulate molecular dynamics, quantum mechanics, or nuclear reactions using Fortran.

2.3. Aerospace and Automotive Engineering

- Model aerodynamics, structural analysis, or propulsion systems in industries that prioritize precision and performance.

2.4. Computational Biology

- Participate in genome analysis or biological simulations.

2.5. Artificial Intelligence (AI) in HPC

- Use Fortran's parallel processing capabilities to accelerate AI models and train machine learning systems at scale.

3. Staying Updated with Fortran Developments

Although Fortran has a rich history, it is a living language with continual updates. Keeping up-to-date ensures you remain competitive and aware of modern tools and practices.

3.1. Follow Fortran Standards

Stay informed about new standards and features. The latest standard, **Fortran 2018**, introduced features like parallel processing with coarrays and better interoperability.

- **Resource:** Visit The ISO Fortran Committee for updates.

3.2. Participate in Fortran Communities

Engage with developers and researchers by joining Fortran forums, mailing lists, or conferences like **SC (Supercomputing)** or **ICCS (International Conference on Computational Science)**.

Popular Communities:

- **Fortran-lang.org**: A hub for modern Fortran enthusiasts.

- **GitHub Repositories**: Contribute to open-source Fortran projects.

- **Stack Overflow**: Ask questions and share knowledge with others.

3.3. Stay Active in HPC Conferences

Attend HPC-focused conferences to stay at the cutting edge of computational science and connect with experts.

4. Additional Resources for Mastery

To deepen your expertise, use the following **resources** to continue learning and applying Fortran:

4.1. Books

- **"Modern Fortran Explained"** by Metcalf, Reid, and Cohen: A comprehensive guide to Fortran's standards.

- **"Numerical Recipes in Fortran"** by Press et al.: A classic for numerical algorithms.

4.2. Online Courses

- **EdX:** Look for HPC-related courses that involve Fortran.

- **Coursera:** Courses on numerical simulations or parallel programming may feature Fortran.

4.3. Documentation

- **Official Fortran Standard Documentation**: Learn directly from the source.

- **Compiler Documentation**: Explore features of compilers like GNU Fortran (gfortran) or Intel Fortran.

4.4. Online Tutorials and Blogs

Follow blogs like **Fortran Monthly** or **Medium articles** by HPC experts.

APPENDICES

Appendix A: Quick Reference to Fortran Syntax

This appendix serves as a handy reference guide to essential Fortran syntax. It is especially useful when you need a quick refresher or are debugging code.

1. Basic Structure of a Fortran Program

```
PROGRAM HelloWorld
    PRINT *, "Hello, World!"
END PROGRAM HelloWorld
```

2. Data Types

- **INTEGER**: Holds whole numbers.

- **REAL**: Holds floating-point numbers.

- **CHARACTER**: Holds strings.

- **LOGICAL**: Holds .TRUE. or .FALSE. values.

- **COMPLEX**: Holds complex numbers.

3. Control Structures

- **IF Statements**:

```
IF (x > 0) THEN
    PRINT *, "Positive"
ELSE
    PRINT *, "Non-positive"
END IF
```

- **DO Loops**:

```
DO i = 1, 10
    PRINT *, i
END DO
```

4. Arrays

```
REAL, DIMENSION(10) :: array
array(1) = 5.0
```

5. Subroutines

```
SUBROUTINE AddNumbers(a, b, result)
   REAL, INTENT(IN) :: a, b
   REAL, INTENT(OUT) :: result
   result = a + b
END SUBROUTINE AddNumbers
```

For more examples, refer to the relevant chapters of this book.

Appendix B: Troubleshooting Common Issues
This appendix provides solutions to frequent problems encountered when coding in Fortran.

1. Compilation Errors

- **Error:** "Unexpected token"

    o **Cause:** Syntax error.

    o **Solution:** Double-check punctuation and capitalization.

- **Error:** "Undefined reference"

    o **Cause:** Missing subroutine or module.

    o **Solution:** Ensure all subroutines and modules are properly declared.

2. Runtime Errors

- **Error:** "Segmentation fault"

- Cause: Accessing out-of-bound array elements.

- Solution: Check array bounds using debugging tools or bounds checking.

- **Error:** "Division by zero"

  - Cause: Division by zero.

  - Solution: Include a conditional check to ensure the denominator is non-zero.

3. Logical Errors

- **Symptom:** Incorrect output despite no errors.

  - Solution: Step through the program with a debugger or use PRINT statements to trace variables.

4. Tips for Debugging

- Use **implicit none** to catch undeclared variables.

- Write modular code to isolate errors.

- Use compiler options like -Wall for GCC to enable warnings.

Appendix C: Glossary of Fortran Terms

This glossary defines key Fortran terms to assist with understanding the language.

- **Argument**: A value passed to a subroutine or function.

- **Array**: A collection of data items stored in contiguous memory.

- **Compiler**: A program that translates Fortran source code into machine code.

- **Module**: A reusable block of code containing subroutines, functions, and variables.

- **Subroutine**: A block of code designed to perform a specific task, similar to a function.

For a complete glossary, revisit relevant chapters.

Appendix D: Resources for Further Learning
Below are some resources to continue your journey in mastering Fortran.

1. Books

- **Modern Fortran Explained** by Metcalf, Reid, and Cohen.

- **Numerical Recipes in Fortran** by Press et al.

2. Online Documentation

- Fortran-lang.org: A hub for modern Fortran.

- GNU Fortran Manual: Official documentation for gfortran.

3. Online Courses

- **Introduction to Fortran for Scientists and Engineers** (Available on platforms like EdX or Coursera).

- **High-Performance Computing with Fortran**: Offered by HPC-focused institutions.

4. Community Forums

- **Fortran-lang Discourse**: A community for Fortran enthusiasts.

- **Stack Overflow**: Find answers to specific coding issues.

5. Conferences and Events

- **Supercomputing (SC)**: Annual conference featuring HPC advancements.

- **International Conference on Computational Science (ICCS)**: Includes sessions on Fortran applications.

Appendix E: Fortran Learning Roadmap for Beginners

Mastering Fortran can seem like a daunting journey, especially for those who are new to programming. However, with the right approach and mindset, you can easily navigate the learning curve and develop a solid understanding of this powerful language. This roadmap will guide you through the essential milestones that will transform you from a complete beginner to a competent Fortran programmer capable of tackling real-world scientific and high-performance computing challenges.

Stage 1: Getting Started with Fortran (Weeks 1–2)

Objective: Understand the basics of programming and get comfortable with the Fortran environment.

1. **Install and Set Up Your Development Environment:**

   - Install a Fortran compiler (e.g., **gfortran**) on your machine.

   - Choose an Integrated Development Environment (IDE) like **VS Code**, **Eclipse**, or **Code::Blocks** for writing and running your code.

- o Test the installation by writing and running your first "Hello, World!" program.

2. **Learn Basic Syntax and Program Structure:**

   - o Understand how a Fortran program is structured: **program block**, **declarations**, **execution section**, and **end program**.

   - o Learn about **statements** and how to **compile** and **execute** a Fortran program.

   - o Explore basic input/output (I/O) using PRINT and READ statements.

   - o Familiarize yourself with basic **data types** in Fortran (integers, real numbers, and characters).

3. **Write Simple Programs:**

   - o Create simple programs that calculate the sum of two numbers or convert units (e.g., inches to centimeters).

Stage 2: Core Concepts (Weeks 3–5)

Objective: Build a strong foundation in key programming concepts, such as variables, control structures, and functions.

1. **Variables and Data Types:**

   - o Learn how to declare and initialize variables.

   - o Explore different data types in detail: **integer**, **real**, **character**, **logical**.

   - o Understand the concept of **arrays** and how they are used to store multiple values of the same type.

2. **Control Structures:**

   ○ Learn how to control program flow using **if/else statements**, **do loops**, and **while loops**.

   ○ Practice writing programs that make decisions (e.g., a program that calculates grades based on score thresholds).

   ○ Explore **nested loops** and conditions to solve more complex problems.

3. **Functions and Subprograms:**

   ○ Learn about **functions** and **subroutines** to break your code into reusable blocks.

   ○ Understand the difference between a **function** and a **subroutine** in Fortran.

   ○ Practice writing simple functions (e.g., a function that calculates the factorial of a number).

4. **Arrays and Data Structures:**

   ○ Learn to create **1D arrays** for storing multiple variables.

   ○ Understand how to manipulate arrays (accessing, updating, and looping through elements).

   ○ Practice with **multidimensional arrays** (e.g., 2D arrays for matrix operations).

Stage 3: Intermediate Programming (Weeks 6–9)

Objective: Start applying your skills to more complex programming challenges and real-world scenarios.

1. **File I/O in Fortran:**

    o Learn how to read from and write to files using **open**, **read**, and **write** commands.

    o Practice with **formatted and unformatted files** (e.g., saving data or reading datasets from a file).

2. **Modular Programming:**

    o Explore **modular programming** techniques by dividing your program into modules for better structure and maintainability.

    o Learn how to use **modules** in Fortran to store reusable code.

3. **Advanced Data Handling:**

    o Learn about **derived data types** (like structures) to create custom data types that hold multiple values of different types.

    o Practice with **array slicing** and **dynamic memory allocation** using **allocatable arrays**.

4. **Error Handling and Debugging:**

    o Understand the importance of error handling with **IF** and **STOP** statements.

    o Practice debugging using print statements and tools like **gdb** for more advanced debugging.

Stage 4: Advanced Concepts (Weeks 10–12)

Objective: Take your Fortran skills to the next level by exploring advanced features used in scientific computing and high-performance computing.

1. **High-Performance Computing with Fortran:**

   o Learn the basics of **parallel programming** with **OpenMP** to make your Fortran code run faster on multi-core processors.

   o Understand **coarrays** in Fortran for parallel computing and explore how they help solve large-scale problems.

2. **Optimization Techniques:**

   o Explore **optimizing your Fortran code** for performance, focusing on memory usage, loop unrolling, and efficient data access patterns.

   o Learn how to use **compiler flags** to improve the performance of your Fortran code.

3. **Interoperability with Other Languages:**

   o Learn how to **link Fortran with C** or use Fortran libraries within other programming languages like Python and MATLAB.

   o Understand the concept of **C interoperability** and **Python wrappers** to extend Fortran's capabilities.

4. **Scientific Libraries and Tools:**

- Familiarize yourself with popular Fortran libraries like **LAPACK** (Linear Algebra), **FFTW** (Fast Fourier Transforms), and **MPI** (Message Passing Interface) for distributed computing.
- Practice solving complex scientific problems using these libraries.

Stage 5: Real-World Application and Projects (Weeks 13–16)

Objective: Apply everything you've learned to real-world projects and prepare for professional use.

1. **Create a Comprehensive Project:**

   - Work on a project like **solving a differential equation**, **simulating physical systems**, or **financial modeling**.
   - Write a detailed report explaining your approach, code, and results.

2. **Collaboration and Version Control:**

   - Learn how to use **Git** for version control and collaborate with others on Fortran projects.
   - Practice committing changes, handling merge conflicts, and maintaining project history.

3. **Capstone Project:**

   - Work on a **Capstone Project** that brings together everything you've learned. This could involve a scientific simulation, a high-performance computing problem, or real-time data analysis.

Final Thoughts and Continued Learning:

Mastering Fortran is a rewarding journey that requires dedication, practice, and continual learning. While this roadmap provides the essential milestones for beginners, true mastery is gained through consistent practice and real-world application. Once you complete this roadmap, you will have the foundation to tackle advanced problems and contribute to scientific or engineering projects.

Remember: **Programming is a marathon, not a sprint.** Embrace each step of your journey, and always seek to expand your knowledge. **The world of Fortran is vast, and the more you explore, the more powerful your skills will become.**

Stay curious. Keep coding. And most importantly, **keep learning.**